HIDDEN MICKEYS GO TO SEA

A Field Guide to the

Disney Cruise Line®'s

Best Kept Secrets

2ND EDITION

Steven M. Barrett

HIDDEN MICKEYS GO TO SEA
A Field Guide to the Disney Cruise Line®'s
Best Kept Secrets
2nd edition

Published by
The Intrepid Traveler
P.O. Box 531
Branford, CT 06405
http://www.intrepidtraveler.com

Copyright ©2013 by Steven M. Barrett
Second Edition
Printed in the U.S.A.
Cover design by Foster & Foster
Interior Design by Starving Artist Design Studio
Library of Congress Card Number: 2012946435
ISBN-13: 978-1-937011-22-2

10 9 8 7 6 5 4 3 2 1

Trademarks, Etc.● ● ● ● ● ● ● ● ● ● ● ●

This book makes reference to various Disney copyrighted characters, trademarks, marks and registered marks owned by The Walt Disney Company and Disney Enterprises, Inc.

All references to these properties are made solely for editorial purposes. Neither the author nor the publisher makes any commercial claim to their use, and neither is affiliated with The Walt Disney Company in any way.

● ●

Also by Steven M. Barrett

Hidden Mickeys:
A Field Guide to Walt Disney World®'s Best Kept Secrets

Disneyland's Hidden Mickeys:
A Field Guide to Disneyland® Resort's Best Kept Secrets

Photo by Vickie Barrett

About the Author............

Steven M. Barrett paid his first visit to Walt Disney World in the late 1980s, after attending a conference in Orlando. He immediately fell under its spell, visiting it twice yearly with family and friends for the next several years, offering touring advice to the less initiated, and reading almost everything written about the WDW theme parks. In 1998, Barrett relocated to the Orlando area from Houston, Texas. He began visiting the WDW parks every chance he got to enjoy the attractions, sample the restaurants, and escort visiting friends and relatives. His interest in Hidden Mickeys led him to take pen in hand and write the Hidden Mickeys field guides to Walt Disney World, Disneyland, and the Disney Cruise Line.

Since Mickey reserves the right to come and go as he—and Disney—pleases, these guides require periodic updates. You hold in your hand the Second Edition of *Hidden Mickeys Go to Sea*, updated to include all the latest Mickey sightings on all four of Disney's cruise ships, as well as its private island, Castaway Cay. Enjoy your hunts!

Dedication •••••••••••••••••••

I dedicate this book to my wife Vickie and our son Steven, who have been tolerant always and supportive most of the time of my passion for Hidden Mickeys. Furthermore, this book would not be possible without the many wonderful Hidden Mickey fans I've met through my website, in the Disney parks, and on the Disney Cruise ships. Thanks to you all.

Acknowledgements••••••••••••

No Hidden Mickey hunter should work alone. While I've spotted most of the Hidden Mickeys in this book on my own, and personally verified every single one of them, finding Hidden Mickeys is an ongoing group effort. I'm indebted to the following dedicated Hidden Mickey lovers for alerting me to a number of Hidden Mickeys I might otherwise have missed. Thanks to each and every one of you for putting me on the track of one or more of these Disney Cruise Line treasures and, in some cases, also helping me verify them. (Names in boldface spotted the most Hidden Mickeys on the ships and on Castaway Cay.) You can find each person's contribution(s) by visiting my website:

www.HiddenMickeyGuy.com

Alex, Amanda, Nancy Ahlsen, Tacey Atkinson, Coleen Bolton, Patti Boyle, Michelle Buchecker, Malcolm Cleveland, **Mary Jo Collins**, Claire Covey, Michael and Lydia Cross, Gary Cruise, **Sharon Dale**, Calvin Dolsay, **Jessica Fortin**, the Frazier family, **Jason Gall**, **Andrew Harris**, Carrie Henderson, **Rick Howard**, Lynette Huey, Andy Jackson, John Koerber, Ronald Laliberte, Ronald Laliberte, Jr., Danielle Lalliberte, **Marc Lorenzo**, Jack Lynch, Linda Mac, Fawn McDonald, Nozomi Muraka, Bill Owen, Carol Ray, Sally-Ann Rose, Kim Schmitt, the Skazick family from the UK, Stu Sumner, **Amanda Tinney**, Vickie (HiddenMickeyGal), Carole and Dennis Wazaney, Max Weitkamp, Jodi Whisenhunt, Don Willis, and Johnson Willis.

Table of Contents ....

True to their name, Hidden Mickeys are elusive. New ones appear from time to time and some old ones disappear (see "Hidden Mickeys Change with Time," page 14). When that happens—and it will—I will let you know on my website:

www.HiddenMickeyGuy.com

So if you can't find a Mickey—or if you're looking for just a few more—be sure to check it out.

Hidden Mickey Mania

● ●

Have you ever marveled at a "Hidden Mickey"? People in the know often shout with glee when they recognize one. Some folks are so involved with discovering them that Hidden Mickeys can be visualized where none actually exist. These outbreaks of Hidden Mickey mania are confusing to the unenlightened. So let's get enlightened!

A Hidden Mickey is a partial or complete impression of Mickey Mouse placed by Walt Disney Imagineers (the creators and builders of the Disney parks) and artists to blend into the designs of Disney attractions, hotels, restaurants, and other areas such as the Disney cruise ships and Disney's private island, Castaway Cay, located in the Bahamas. The most common Hidden Mickey form is the tri-circle Mickey silhouette: three circles that form Mickey's round head and adjoining round ears as seen from the front. I call this image the "classic Mickey." Other forms include a side or oblique (usually three-quarter) profile of Mickey's face and head, a side profile of his entire body, a full-body frontal silhouette, a detailed picture of his face or body, or a three-dimensional Mickey. Sometimes, just his gloves, handprints, shoes, or ears appear. Even his name or initials in unusual places may qualify as Hidden Mickeys. And don't forget other Hidden Characters such as Minnie, Donald Duck, Goofy, Daisy Duck, and Tinker Bell; they, too, are part of the Hidden Mickey family. Some images are more hidden than others and thus harder to discover. However, anyone can have fun finding Hidden Mickeys!

Hidden Mickeys probably started as an inside joke among the Imagineers. According to Disney guru Jim Hill (www.JimHillMedia.com), Hidden Mickeys originated in the late 1970s or early 1980s, when Disney was building Epcot. Disney management wanted to restrict Disney characters like Mickey and Minnie to the Magic Kingdom Park. However, the Imagineers designing Epcot couldn't resist slipping Mickey into the new park, and thus "Hidden Mickeys" were born. Guests and "Cast Members" (Disney employees) started spotting them and the concept took on a life of its own. Today, Hidden Mickeys are anticipated in any new Disney construction, and Hidden Mickey fans can't wait to find them.

The sport of finding Hidden Mickeys is catching on and adds even more interest to an already fun-filled Disney cruise. This book is your "field guide" to more than 300 Hidden Mickeys on the Disney Cruise Line ships and Castaway Cay. To add to the fun, instead of just describing them, I've organized them into five scavenger hunts, one for each of the four cruise ships and one for Castaway Cay. The hunts are designed for maximum efficiency, starting on the upper decks on the ships and at the dock end of Castaway Cay. Follow the Clues and you will find the best Hidden Mickeys the Disney Cruise Line has to offer. If you have trouble spotting a particular Hidden Mickey (some are extraordinarily well camouflaged!) you can turn to the Hints at the end of each scavenger hunt for a fuller description.

Scavenger Hunting for Hidden Mickeys

To have the most fun and find the most Mickeys, follow these tips:

★ "Clues" and "Hints"
Clues in each hunt will guide you to the Hidden Mickey(s). If you have trouble spotting them, you can turn to the Hints at the end of the hunt for a fuller description. The Clues and Hints are numbered consecutively, that is, Hint 1 goes with Clue 1; so it's easy to find the right Hint if you need it.

★ Scoring
All Hidden Mickeys are fun to find, but all Hidden Mickeys aren't the same. Some

are easier to locate than others. I assign point values to Hidden Mickeys, identifying them as easy to spot (a value of 1 point) to difficult to find the first time (5 points). I also consider the complexity and uniqueness of the image: the more complex or unique the Hidden Mickey, the higher the point value.

★ Playing the game
You can hunt solo or with others, competitively or just for fun. There's room to tally your score in the guide. Families with young children may want to focus on one- and two-point Mickeys that the little ones will have no trouble spotting. (Of course, little ones tend to be sharp-eyed; so they may spot familiar shapes before you do in some of the more complex patterns.) Or you may want to split your party into teams and see who can rack up the most points (in which case, you'll probably want to have a book for each team).

Of course, you don't have to play the game at all. You can simply look for Hidden Mickeys in areas as you come to them (see "Finding Hidden Mickeys Without Scavenger Hunting," below).

★ Playing fair
Be considerate of other guests. Many Hidden Mickeys are in restaurants and shops. Ask a Cast Member's permission before searching inside sit-down restaurants, and avoid the busy mealtime hours unless you are one of the diners. Tell the Cast Members and other guests who see you looking around what you're up to, so they can share in the fun.

Finding Hidden Mickeys Without Scavenger Hunting

If scavenger hunts don't appeal to you, you don't have to use them. You can find Hidden Mickeys in the specific areas you visit by using the *Index to Mickey's Hiding Places* in the back of this book.

Caution: You won't find every area of the ships or island in the *Index*. Only those with confirmed Hidden Mickeys are included in this guide.

Hidden Mickeys, "Gray Zone" Mickeys, Wishful Thinking

The classic (three-circle) Mickeys are the most controversial, for good reason. Much debate surrounds the gathering of circular forms throughout Disney areas. Three-circle configurations occur spontaneously in art and nature, as in collections of grapes, tomatoes, pumpkins, bubbles, oranges, cannonballs, and the like. It may be difficult to attribute a random "classic Mickey" configuration of circles to a deliberate Imagineer design.

So which groupings of three circles qualify as Hidden Mickeys as opposed to wishful thinking? (My neighbor, Lew Brooks, calls the latter "two-beer Mickeys.") Unfortunately, no master list of actual or "Imagineer-approved" Hidden Mickeys exists. Purists demand that a true classic Hidden Mickey should have proper proportions and positioning. The round head must be larger than the ear circles (so that three equal circles in the proper alignment would not qualify as a Hidden Mickey). The head and ears must be touching and in perfect position for Mickey's head and ears.

On the other hand, Disney's recent mantra is: "If the guest thinks it's a Hidden Mickey, then by golly it is one!" Of course, I appreciate Disney's respect for their guests' opinions. However, when the subject is Hidden Mickeys, let's apply some guidelines. My own criteria are looser than the purists' but stricter than the "anything goes" Disney approach.

My Classic Mickey Criteria

I use a few guidelines to help me discriminate between a classic (three-circle) Hidden Mickey and any random image of three circles that just happen to be close together. To be classified as a true classic Mickey, the three circles should meet the following criteria:

 1. Purposeful (sometimes you can sense that the circles were placed on purpose).

2. Proportionate sizes (head larger than and some-what proportionate to the ears).

3. Round or roundish circles.

4. The ears don't touch each other and they are above — not beside — the head.

5. The head and ears touch or are close to touching.

6. The grouping of circles is exceptional or unique in appearance.

7. The circles are hidden, or somewhat hidden, and are not simply decorative or or an obvious part of the décor.

Hidden Mickeys vs. Decorative Mickeys

Some Mickeys are purely decorative; they were placed in plain sight to enhance the décor and add to the guest's fun. For example, in a restaurant, I con-sider a pat of butter shaped like Mickey's head to be a decorative (aka décor) Mickey. The same is true of many paintings, drawings, and statuettes of Mickey and other characters that you'll find decorating both the public areas and staterooms on the ships. Such images are so obvious to the viewer that they don't qualify as "hidden" —with one exception:

If most people don't notice the image, I consider it a "Hidden Mickey" even when it is in plain sight. A good example is the Hidden Mickey of Clue 22 in both the *Disney Magic* and *Disney Wonder* scavenger hunts (see *Chapters Four* and *Five*).

Truly Hidden Mickeys

Some Mickeys are truly hidden, that is, not visible or accessible to the guest. For example, they may be located behind the scenes and accessible only to Cast Members. You won't find such images in this field guide. I only include Hidden Mickeys guests can find.

Hidden Mickeys Change with Time

Hidden Mickeys can change or be accidentally removed over time, by the process of nature or by the continual cleaning and refurbishing that goes on in Disney areas. While that can mean saying goodbye to an old friend, it also means that new Hidden Mickeys are continually being created by the Imagineers. Which means we'll never run out of new Hidden Mickeys to search for.

My Selection Process

I trust you've concluded by now that Hidden Mickey Science is an evolving specialty. Which raises the question, how did I choose the 300-plus Hidden Mickeys in the scavenger hunts in this guide?

I compiled my list of Hidden Mickeys from all resources to which I had access: my own sightings, friends, family, Cast Members, websites, and books. (Cast Members in each specific area usually—but not always!—know where some Hidden Mickeys are located.) Then I embarked on my own hunts, and I took along friends or family to verify my sightings. The scavenger hunts include only those Hidden Mickeys that meet my criteria (see above), are visible to the general guest, and that I could personally verify.

While it is likely that one or more of the Hidden Mickeys described in this book will disappear over time, I have tried to lessen the odds of that happening by purposely leaving out the Mickey images that are most likely to change over time (such as some Hidden Mickeys on menus, in store display windows, or inside staterooms) unless they've been around awhile. I'll try to let you know when I discover that a Hidden Mickey has disappeared for good by posting the information on my website:

www.HiddenMickeyGuy.com

If you find one missing before I do, please email me care of my website to let me know.

I have enjoyed finding each and every Hidden Mickey in this book. I'm certain I'll find more as time goes by, and I hope you can spot new Hidden Mickeys as you sail the seas and enjoy Disney's private island.

Happy Hunting!

— *Steve Barrett*

Port Canaveral Check-In Terminal Hidden Mickey Hunt

If your ship leaves from Port Canaveral, you can hunt for Hidden Mickeys while you wait to check in.

Clue 1: Study chairs inside the Port Canaveral check-in terminal for Hidden Mickeys.
1 point

Clue 2: Find Hidden Mickeys in windows inside the terminal.
3 points

Check-In Terminal Hints

Hint 1: Chairs with classic Mickey holes in the upper backs are placed in various seating areas inside the terminal.

Hint 2: The Disney Cruise Line logo features a classic Mickey in the center of a waving banner. These logos decorate several areas of the check-in terminal, including the chairs. Look closely at the terminal's round windows to spot the logo classic Mickey painted like very faint stained glass on the terminal's round windows. Look closely. The paint is applied so subtly that these logos count as Hidden Mickeys.

Disney Dream™ Scavenger Hunt

• •

Note: This Hunt includes only those places that harbor confirmed Hidden Mickeys. So if the area you're looking in isn't included, Mickey isn't hiding there. Or if he is, I haven't yet spotted him.

★ Go to Guest Services on **Deck 3 midship** and find out when "Open House" is scheduled for the Edge club (for tweens ages 11 to 14) and Disney's Oceaneer Club (for ages 3 to 12). Plan your visits accordingly. You can also enter anytime if you have a child registered in the venue.

★ Stop by a **Deck 5 midship** registration desk and sign up for the Midship Detective Agency Game, in which you'll interact with wall paintings around the ship. Hidden Mickeys are in some of these interactive windows. For purposes of this Hidden Mickey Scavenger Hunt, choose "The Case of the Stolen Puppies" game if it's available. While you're at it, look for some Hidden Mickeys on the introductory computer screens as you complete the registration!

Clue 1: Be alert for Hidden Mickey gears.
4 points

Clue 2: Look quickly for a Mickey key.
3 points

Clue 3: Study the desktop for a blue full-body Mickey.
5 points

★ Walk to Goofy's Mini Golf on **Deck 13 aft**.

Clue 4: Don't miss Goofy's "Lesson One" diagram for four Hidden Mickeys. (You'll also find these classic Mickeys on the golf course.)
4 points for all four

Clue 5: Check out the golf bags to find two Hidden Mickeys.
2 points for both

Clue 6: Admire a coffee cup at the end of the course.
3 points

Clue 7: Look up to find the time.
2 points

Clue 8: Spot Mickey around the basketball court.
1 point

★ Take the aft elevator or nearby stairs down to **Deck 12 aft**.

Clue 9: Study the large, round, lighted map behind the receptionist counter for the Palo and Remy restaurants.
3 points

★ Enter the **Meridian Lounge** or return later when it's open.

Clue 10: Look up for Mickey.
3 points

★ Go outside and walk **toward midship**.

Clue 11: Gaze down at a big Mickey profile.
2 points

Clue 12: Now look for Donald's profile. (This image may be easier to spot from Deck 11.)
4 points

Clue 13: Search for Donald midship.
3 points

★ At Deck 12 midship, walk the stairs or take the elevator to Edge, the ship's tween club, at "Open House" time. You can enter anytime if you have a child registered here. Edge is on **Deck 13**.

Clue 14: Check out the walls.
2 points

Clue 15: Look at the floors.
2 points

★ Return to Deck 12 and walk to the **Deck 11 forward stairs**.

Clue 16: Gaze into the nearby hallway at the guest room doors.
2 points

Clue 17: When you have the opportunity, look down in guest room hallways.
2 points

Clue 18: Admire a painting on a wall nearby for a Hidden Mickey.
3 points

★ Walk to Nemo's Reef on **Deck 11 midship**.

Clue 19: Search for Mickey on the floor.
3 points

★ Enter Cabanas restaurant on **Deck 11 aft**. If it's closed, return later at mealtime.

Clue 20: Study the window areas for Hidden Mickeys.
2 points

Clue 21: Admire the drinking glasses.
2 points

★ Walk to the **Deck 10 forward** elevator area.

Clue 22: Study the vicinity of the elevator buttons and directional arrows.
3 points for spotting Mickey in both areas

Clue 23: Press for an elevator and look down for a Hidden Mickey when the door opens.
2 points

Clue 24: Enjoy an interactive painting near these elevators. Stand in front of the painting, and it will come to life! Watch closely for a classic Hidden Mickey.
5 points

★ Descend to the **Deck 8 forward** elevator area.

Clue 25: Check out the framed interactive paintings near the elevators. (Just standing in front of some of these windows activates them.)
5 points for two

★ Now pull out your Midship Detective Agency game card and watch one of these paintings come to life!

Clue 26: Look for a Hidden Mickey that appears at the beginning of the game.
5 points

★ Go down to **Deck 5 forward** and walk toward midship.

Clue 27: Admire Hidden Mickeys below your feet (outside and inside the theatre).
2 points

Clue 28: Look at the hallway walls.
1 point

★ Enter the **Buena Vista Theatre** (or return later for a scheduled show or movie).

Clue 29: Find classic Mickeys along the sides of the theatre.
2 points

Clue 30: Look up for Mickey.
3 points

Clue 31: Check your seat.
1 point

★ Exit the Buena Vista Theatre and walk **toward midship**.

20

Clue 32: Near the Deck 5 midship elevators, find a painting with Hidden Characters.
5 points for five images

Clue 33: Near the Deck 5 Port Adventures desk, look around for two tiny red and black classic Mickeys on the wall.
5 points for both

Clue 34: Also near the Port Adventures desk, search for a classic Mickey on a ship.
4 points

Clue 35: Admire the chandelier hanging in the atrium.
3 points

★ Enter **Disney's Oceaneer Club** at the "Open House" time. (You can enter anytime if you have a child 3 to 12 years old who is registered in the Club.)

Clue 36: Search for Disney characters in points of light.
5 points for two or more

Clue 37: Study the walls of the central room for Hidden Mickeys.
5 points for one or more

Clue 38: Look for Mickey in Andy's Room.
2 points

Clue 39: Glance inside the restrooms (or ask your child to look inside) for Hidden Mickeys.
1 point

Clue 40: Watch the Activities Board on the wall in front of the Club.
2 points

★ Stop in front of the entrance to **Disney's Oceaneer Lab**.

Clue 41: Search the displays behind the entrance gates for a classic Mickey.
4 points

★ Walk to the **Deck 5 aft** elevator area.

★ Use your Midship Detective Agency game card to activate one of the paintings by the Deck 5 aft elevators.

Clue 42: As "The Case of the Stolen Puppies" game starts, keep your eyes peeled for a tiny classic Mickey. It's in the frame with the newspaper at the top that features the headline "Fur Flies In ...". (*Note:* This same Hidden Mickey may appear in other interactive paintings around the ship).
5 points

★ Walk down to **Deck 4 aft**.

Clue 43: Admire the inside of the Pink Lounge and then look around for Hidden Mickeys.
4 points

★ Stroll into **D Lounge midship**.

Clue 44: Look up for Mickey.
3 points

Clue 45: Study the floor.
3 points

Clue 46: Search the hall outside D Lounge.
3 points

★ Walk **forward on Deck 4**.

Clue 47: Check out some of the lower-deck elevators (such as these on Deck 4 forward) for Mickey above the doors.
2 points

★ Enter the **Walt Disney Theatre** at a show time of your choice.

Clue 48: Study the inside of the theatre for a Hidden Mickey on both sides of the stage.
3 points

Clue 49: Look along the walls inside the Walt Disney Theatre.
2 points

★ Go to **Deck 3 forward**. Look around Mickey's Mainsail shop

Clue 50: Peer at the hall windows of Mickey's Mainsail for Mickey.
3 points

Clue 51: Scan a rear window of the shop for Mickey.
2 points

Clue 52: Look for Mickey in the designs on the shop's walls and merchandise stands.
2 points

Clue 53: Gaze up for Mickey.
2 points

★ Go across the hall to the **Sea Treasures** shop.

Clue 54: Find Mickey in the shop design.
2 points

★ Stroll to the huge atrium, **Deck 3 midship**.

Clue 55: Glance all around the atrium for outlines of Disney characters.
2 points

Clue 56: Look for more Disney characters in relief.
2 points

Clue 57: Search the scrollwork over the elevator shafts for a classic Mickey.
3 points

Clue 58: Now look lower in the elevator scrollwork for another Mickey image.
3 points

★ Enter the **Royal Palace** restaurant. (You can always enter at your assigned mealtime).

Clue 59: Find classic Mickey images in paintings. (Be considerate of servers and other guests as you search for them here and in other restaurants.)
3 points

★ Walk **aft to Animator's Palate** restaurant. (You can always enter at your assigned mealtime).

Clue 60: Study the mural just inside the entrance.
3 points

Clue 61: Glance down at the tile.
2 points

Clue 62: Admire the carpet inside the restaurant.
1 point

Clue 63: Don't miss the breadbasket and dishes!
3 points for both

Clue 64: Check out your server's clothing.
2 points

★ Walk down to **Deck 2 midship**.

Clue 65: Observe the elevator scrollwork.
3 points

Clue 66: Approach the Enchanted Garden restaurant and spot a Hidden Mickey.
3 points

★ Check out **your stateroom** for Hidden Mickeys. (Mickey images can be found in many objects in your stateroom.)

Clue 67: Study various knobs.
2 points

Clue 68: Admire light fixtures.
2 points

Clue 69: Look in the bathroom.

2 points

24

★ **Remy** restaurant bonus points opportunity

Clue 70: If you eat in Remy, look around for several Hidden Remys!
(5 bonus points for images in five different places)

Now total your score.

Total Points for
the Disney Dream =

```




```

How'd you do?
Up to 78 points – Bronze
79 to 154 points – Silver
155 points and over - Gold
194 points – Perfect Score

(You may have done even better if you earned bonus points for Hidden Mickeys you found in your state-room and Remy restaurant.)

Notes

● ● ● ● ● ● ● ● ● ● ● ● ●
**Caution:
Don't peek at this
section unless you
really want help!**
● ● ● ● ● ● ● ● ● ● ● ● ●

Deck 5 midship

- Detective Game Registration Desk

Hint 1: During registration for the "Midship Detective Agency" game, a desktop with objects on it appears on the computer screen. A classic Mickey made of gears is drawn on the right side of a page on the desk entitled "For Review & Comment."

Hint 2: A small gold key on the right upper desktop area has Mickey ears.

Hint 3: A tiny, light blue full-body Mickey Mouse hides at the top of the first note of a pad of white sticky notes on the right side of the desktop.

Deck 13 aft

– Goofy's Sports Deck

Hint 4: A diagram entitled "Lesson One: The Proper Stance" is on a wall before the first hole of Goofy's Mini Golf. Max's four footprints on the diagram each sport a classic Mickey. You can also find these classic Mickeys inside Max's footprints on the actual golf course.

Hint 5: Light blue classic Mickeys are on patches on Goofy's green golf bags at the beginning and end of the nine-hole miniature golf course.

Hint 6: A classic Mickey made of white swirls is in a blue coffee cup at the beginning of the ninth hole.

Hint 7: The hour and minute hands of the clocks above you near Goofy's Mini Golf Course are Mickey's hands.

Hint 8: Large white classic Mickeys adorn the upper part of the support structure for the net that encloses the basketball court on Goofy's Sports Deck.

Deck 12 aft

- Meridian Lounge area

Hint 9: On the front of the huge lighted circular map on the wall behind the receptionist counter for Palo and Remy restaurants, you'll find a classic Mickey impression in the middle circle of the metal star.

Hint 10: A classic Mickey impression is also in the middle circle of the metal star on the large round light fixture that is hanging from the ceiling in the center of the Meridian Lounge.

Deck 12 midship

Hint 11: Visible from Deck 12 near midship, a colorful three-quarter profile of Mickey Mouse's face is on the bottom of Mickey's (children's) Pool. His big hand holds up a water slide.

Hint 12: A full-body image of Donald Duck is on the bottom of Donald's (family) pool. He's difficult to spot if the water is swirling around! In fact, you may have to walk down to Deck 11 and stand right by the pool to find him.

Hint 13: Donald Duck crashes headfirst into the port side of the ship's funnel midship. You can see his legs, rump, and life preserver. Hope he's okay!

Deck 13 forward funnel

- Edge

Hint 14: Classic Mickeys are scattered over the wallpaper inside the Edge club.

Hint 15: Classic Mickeys appear inside some of the circles in both the turquoise and red carpets inside the club.

Deck 11 forward

Hint 16: On the upper decks, guest room doorbells are surrounded by silver metal classic Mickeys.

Hint 17: Red classic Mickeys hide in the corners of some of the guest hallway carpet designs.

Stairwell between Decks 11 and 10 forward

Hint 18: A cloud classic Mickey image is at the upper left of a painting that's hanging on the wall about halfway down the stairwell as you walk toward Deck 10. Look for the painting that includes a shoreline with palm trees.

Deck 11 midship

- Nemo's Reef

Hint 19: A classic Mickey made of three white circles hides on the port side floor of

29

HINTS HINTS HINTS HINTS HINTS HINTS HINTS HINTS HINTS HINTS HINTS HINTS HINTS HINTS HINTS

Nemo's Reef. The circles in this image are touching and proportioned properly. (Some of the other circles on the floor here come close to forming classic Hidden Mickeys but don't quite meet the criteria (see *Chapter One)*.

Deck 11 aft

- Cabanas restaurant

Hint 20: Inside the restaurant near the bottom of the window posts, silver classic Mickeys secure the chains of the window coverings.

Hint 21: Subtle classic Mickeys are scattered over drinking glasses.

Deck 10 forward

Hint 22: Examine the tops of both the metal discs that contain the elevator buttons and the metal strips that frame the elevator's directional arrows. Small classic Mickey impressions are on both. You'll find these images on elevators all over the ship.

Hint 23: Check the floor of the elevator. A silver classic Mickey hides on a silver strip under each elevator's door.

Hint 24: On the wall near the Deck 10 forward elevators, a pink octopus appears at one point in an interactive painting featuring Ariel. Check the octopus's head. A classic Mickey formed of bumps rests on its upper right side.

Deck 8 forward

Hint 25: On the wall near the Deck 8 forward elevators, look for the painting of a snorkeling Goofy entitled "Mexican Riviera." You'll find a classic Hidden Mickey hides on the side of a Disney Cruise ship at the top of the painting. (A saluting décor Mickey Mouse is on the front of the ship). Nearby, in a painting entitled "Disney Cruise Line – Alaska," white classic

Mickeys are on the funnels of the ship that moves across the bottom of the painting.

Hint 26: When your detective game card activates the "Disney Cruise Line" painting, a classic Mickey made of orange gears appears as the game begins.

Deck 5 forward

- Buena Vista Theatre

Hint 27: Blue classic Mickeys are in the hallway carpet outside the Buena Vista Theatre. (This carpet design also appears inside the theatre.)

Hint 28: Light brown classic Mickey "hats" (classic Mickeys with the "head" circle cut in half) lie low on the hallway wall outside the Buena Vista Theatre.

Hint 29: Inside the Buena Vista Theatre, classic Mickeys are in the ornamental scrollwork design on light fixtures along the side walls.

Hint 30: Classic Mickeys ring the small central part of the huge star-shaped light fixture hanging from the center of the theatre ceiling.

Hint 31: Small white classic Mickeys are repeated in the pattern of the theatre seats.

Deck 5 midship

Hint 32: Near the Deck 5 midship elevators, a Disney ship in a painting hosts Hidden Images, including Daisy Duck, Pluto, Minnie and Mickey on a jet ski, and a tiny black classic Hidden Mickey. You can also see a saluting décor Mickey on the front of the ship.

- Port Adventures desk area

Hint 33: In an interactive map of the Caribbean Sea on a wall near the Deck 5 Port

Adventures desk, a red classic Mickey sits on Castaway Cay and a black classic Mickey is in the middle of the compass at the lower left of the map.

Hint 34: Across from the Deck 5 Port Adventures desk, a painting with the Queen Minnie ship has a classic Mickey on the side of the cabin at the middle of the ship.

Hint 35: Small classic Mickeys are near the top of the multicolored atrium chandelier.

- Disney's Oceaneer Club

Hint 36: Inside Disney's Oceaneer Club, Peter Pan and Tinker Bell, among other characters, are traced in points of light on the ceiling.

Hint 37: Faint, tiny classic Hidden Mickeys lie on the "Memory Wall." Look for the wall with numbers. It's on the left side (as you enter) of the club's large central room.

Hint 38: A full-body Mickey hides on the face of a green watch that hangs on the right wall of Andy's Room, which is to the right of the central room (as you enter).

Hint 39: On the wall above the restroom sinks, large round mirrors (Mickey "heads") are topped with two round lights ("ears") to form classic Mickeys. (Many restrooms throughout the ship have classic Mickey mirrors. Some have lights for ears, while others are topped with smaller round mirrors.)

Hint 40: White classic Mickeys move in and out on the digital Activities Board on the wall in front of the Club. (You can spot similar white classic Mickeys on Activities Boards for other clubs around the ship.)

- Disney's Oceaneer Lab

Hint 41: Look for a white ship's wheel about halfway up the rear wall in the middle of the display area behind the entrance gates. A small red classic Mickey hides in the middle of the wheel.

Deck 5 aft

Hint 42: Near the Deck 5 aft elevators, a tiny upside-down classic Mickey appears in an interactive painting activated by your game card. It's in the frame with the newspaper at the top that features the headline "Fur Flies In … ." Look for this Hidden Mickey as you move your magnifying glass around the painting. It will appear under your magnifying glass at the lower right of the painting to the left of the words "Cove Cafe."

Deck 4 aft

- Pink Lounge

Hint 43: Circles form classic Mickeys in various areas of the carpet inside Pink. In these images, part of Mickey's "head" is obscured by other carpet colors, but once you spot the image, you won't have any trouble identifying it as a classic Mickey.

Deck 4 midship

- D Lounge

Hint 44: Some of the large circular light fixtures on the ceiling of D Lounge form classic Mickeys.

Hint 45: Several of the carpet sections have circles of brown, black, or white. Some groups of circles form classic Mickeys with light brown Mickey "heads."

Hint 46: In the hall carpet outside D Lounge, circles made of swirls form classic Mickeys.

Deck 4 forward

- Elevator area

Hint 47: Above some of the ship's elevator

doors, such as these on Deck 4 forward, Mickey's hand points to the deck levels.

- Walt Disney Theatre

Hint 48: Inside the Walt Disney Theatre, which occupies both Deck 4 and Deck 3 forward, look for brightly lit classic Mickeys about halfway up each side of the stage. Psst! They hide within the lighted designs. (You can also see a décor Mickey made entirely of light.)

Hint 49: Also inside the theatre, classic Mickeys are repeated in the ornamental design of the friezes along the walls, above the stage, and under the railings.

Deck 3 forward

- Mickey's Mainsail shop

Hint 50: A small side-profile Mickey sits in a boat under the "M" of the word "MainSail" in the Mickey's Mainsail logo painted in white on the windows facing the corridor along the outer wall of the shop.

Hint 51: Inside, at the rear of the shop, small classic Mickeys hide in the round perimeters of the porthole windows.

Hint 52: Mickey hats, with incomplete swirls for ears, are in the design of the friezes high on the shop walls and at the top of some merchandise stands inside Mickey's Mainsail.

Hint 53: White classic Mickeys lie along the side and at the bottom of the shop's circular ceiling chandelier.

- Sea Treasures shop

Hint 54: Classic Mickeys hide in the design of both the friezes high up on the walls near the shop's ceiling. and atop some of its merchandise stands.

34

Deck 3 midship

- Atrium

Hint 55: Outside Royal Palace restaurant, Disney characters (Minnie, Goofy, and so on) are repeated in the design of the staircase railings.

Hint 56: Disney characters are also featured in relief on the gold horizontal friezes on the edges of the walkways around the atrium on Decks 4 and 5. You can see them well when standing in front of Royal Palace restaurant.

Hint 57: Classic Mickeys hide near the top of the ornamental scrollwork adorning the elevator shafts facing the atrium lobby.

Hint 58: Side-profile Mickeys are at the bottom of this same ornamental scrollwork.

- Royal Palace restaurant

Hint 59: Paintings of Disney characters (Snow White, Belle, and so on) are on the left wall inside the Royal Palace. White classic Mickey circles (the "ears" are incomplete) lie just above the heads of the characters.

Deck 3 aft

- Animator's Palate restaurant

Hint 60: Just inside the entrance to Animator's Palate, a mural features a series of drawings of a Dalmation running and jumping. Black spots on the dog's right upper leg form classic Mickeys at times. (The "Mickey" spots look different in each depiction, depending on the dog's position, so some form more convincing Hidden Mickeys than others.)

Hint 61: Also just inside the entrance, white classic Mickeys are sprinkled around the large circle of dark floor tile.

Hint 62: The restaurant's carpet hides classic Mickeys.

Hint 63: Some of the circles in the wire breadbasket form classic Mickeys, and classic Mickeys also decorate the right side of the dishes.

Hint 64: The servers wear classic Mickey belt buckles!

Deck 2 midship

- Elevator area

Hint 65: Classic Mickeys rest in the scrollwork of the elevator shafts.

- Outside Enchanted Garden restaurant

Hint 66: Classic Mickeys hide in the ornamental metalwork of the restaurant's entrance gate.

Inside your stateroom

Hint 67: The metal knobs on your stateroom's desk and closets have classic Mickeys in the middle.

Hint 68: Classic Mickey holes embellish the metal bands around various lamps and light fixtures.

Hint 69: A rope design in the shower curtain forms classic Mickeys. (Similar rope-design classic Mickeys hide on the rolling housekeeping bags in the guest hallways.)

Deck 12 aft

- Remy restaurant

Hint 70: Images of Remy are scattered around the restaurant. They're in the fabric of the dining booths, in the gold strips decorating the walls, in the woodwork of a mirror, and in the woodwork on the back of chairs. A full-body glass Remy hides atop a lighting fixture.

CHAPTER 3

Disney Fantasy™
Scavenger Hunt

Note: This Hunt includes only those places that harbor confirmed Hidden Mickeys. So if the area you're looking in isn't included, Mickey isn't hiding there. Or if he is, I haven't yet spotted him.

★ Go to Guest Services on **Deck 3 midship** and find out when "Open House" is scheduled for Edge (the club for tweens ages 11 to 14), Disney's Oceaneer Club (for ages 3 to 12), and Disney's Oceaneer Lab (also for ages 3 to 12). Plan your visits accordingly. You can enter anytime if you have a child registered in the club.

★ Stop by a **Deck 5 midship** registration desk and sign up for the "Midship Detective Agency" game, in which you'll interact with wall paintings around the ship. Hidden Mickeys are in some of these interactive windows. For purposes of this Hidden Mickey Scavenger Hunt, choose "The Case of the Stolen Puppies" game if it's available. While you're at it, look for some Hidden Mickeys on the introductory computer screens as you complete the registration!

Clue 1: Be alert for Hidden Mickey gears.
4 points

Clue 2: Look quickly for a Mickey key.
3 points

Clue 3: Study the desktop for a blue full-body Mickey.
5 points

★ Walk to Goofy Golf on **Deck 13 aft**.

Clue 4: Check out the golf bags to spot two
Hidden Mickeys.
2 points for spotting both

Clue 5: Don't miss classic Mickeys on the putting surface along the golf course.
2 points

Clue 6: Admire a coffee cup at the end of the course.
3 points

Clue 7: Spot Mickey around the basketball court.
1 point

★ Take the aft elevator or nearby stairs down to **Deck 12**.

Clue 8: Study the large, round lighted map behind the receptionist counter for Palo and Remy restaurants.
3 points

★ Enter the **Meridian Lounge** or return later when it's open.

Clue 9: Look up for Mickey.
3 points

★ Go outside to Deck 12 aft and walk **toward midship**.

Clue 10: Gaze down at a big Mickey profile.
2 points

Clue 11: Search for Donald midship.
3 points

★ At Deck 12 midship, walk the stairs or take the elevator to Edge, the ship's tween club, at "Open House" time (or anytime it's open if you have a child registered there). Edge is on **Deck 13** in the forward funnel.

Clue 12: Check out the walls.
2 points

Clue 13: Look at the floors.
2 points

38 ★ Return to Deck 12 and walk to the **Deck 11 forward stairs**.

Clue 14: Find a tiny blue Hidden Mickey near the Deck 11 elevators.
3 points

Clue 15: Gaze into the nearby hallway at the guest room doors.
2 points

Clue 16: When you have the opportunity, look down in guest room hallways.
2 points

★ Walk to **Deck 11 midship**.

Clue 17: Look up to find the time.
2 points

★ Now walk to **Nemo's Reef**.

Clue 18: Search for two Mickeys on the floor.
5 points for finding both

Clue 19: Find Mickey on Mr. Ray! (If you're not with your child and not in your bathing suit, ask a Cast Member if you can return later when the water is off to look for this Hidden Mickey).
5 points

★ Enter Cabanas restaurant on **Deck 11 aft**. If it's closed, return later at mealtime.

Clue 20: Look near the seats for Mickey.
2 points

Clue 21: Study the window areas for Hidden Mickeys.
2 points

Clue 22: Admire the drinking glasses.
2 points

★ Walk to the **Deck 10 forward** elevator area.

Clue 23: Press for an elevator and look down for a Hidden Mickey when the door opens.
2 points

Clue 24: Enjoy an interactive painting near these elevators. Stand in front of the painting, and it will come to life! Watch closely for a classic Hidden Mickey.
5 points

★ Descend to the stairwell **between Decks 7 and 6 forward**.

Clue 25: Study the frame of a painting on the wall.
4 points

★ Go down to **Deck 5** forward and walk **toward midship**.

Clue 26: Admire Hidden Mickeys below your feet (outside and inside the theatre).
2 points

Clue 27: Look at the hallway walls.
1 point

★ Enter the **Buena Vista Theatre** (or return later for a scheduled show or movie).

Clue 28: Find classic Mickeys along the sides of the theatre.
2 points

Clue 29: Look up for Mickey.
3 points

Clue 30: Check your seat.
1 point

★ Exit the Buena Vista Theatre and walk **toward midship**.

Clue 31: Look around for a picture on the wall with tiny red and black classic Mickeys.
5 points for spotting two

Clue 32: Admire the chandelier hanging in the atrium.
3 points

★ Enter **Disney's Oceaneer Club** at the "Open House" time (or any time it is open if you have a child registered in the Club.

Clue 33: Search for Disney characters in points of light.
5 points for 2 or more

Clue 34: Look for Mickey in Andy's Room.
2 points

Clue 35: Watch the Activities Board on the wall in front of the Club.
2 points

★ Step into **Disney's Oceaneer Lab** at the "Open House" time. (You can enter any time if you have a child registered here.)

Clue 36: Search the displays behind the entrance gates for a classic Mickey.
3 points

★ Walk to the **Deck 5 aft** elevator area.

Clue 37: Use your Midship Detective Agency game card to activate one of the paintings by the Deck 5 aft elevators. As "The Case of the Stolen Puppies" game starts, keep your eyes peeled for a classic Mickey. (*Note:* This same Hidden Mickey appears in other interactive paintings around the ship.)
5 points

Clue 38: Stay alert for a tiny classic Mickey as the interactive game progresses. You'll find it in the frame with the newspaper at the top with a headline "Fur Flies In ... ." (Psst! This same Hidden Mickey may appear in other interactive paintings around the ship.)
5 points

★ Walk down to **Deck 4 aft** and check out Skyline Lounge (or return later when it's open).

Clue 39: Watch for Mickey in the scenes of London on the wall screens.
5 points

★ Stroll into D Lounge **Deck 4 midship**.

Clue 40: Look up for Mickey in D Lounge.
3 points

Clue 41: Study the floor.
3 points

★ Cross through **Shutters** at Deck 4 midship.

Clue 42: Stop for Hidden Mickeys in the ornamental design. (Decorative Mickey images are scattered around Shutters as well.)
4 points for two different Hidden Mickeys

★ Walk **forward** on Deck 4 or Deck 3.

★ Enter the **Walt Disney Theatre** at a show time of your choice.

Clue 43: Study the inside of the theatre for Hidden Mickeys above, in front of, and to the side of the stage.
5 points for spotting three or more

Clue 44: Now look for Hidden Mickeys along the theatre's interior railings and balcony.
3 points for two or more

Clue 45: Check out the speakers for Hidden Mickeys.
5 points for two

★ Go to the **Deck 3 forward** elevators.

Clue 46: Check out some of the lower-deck elevators (such as these) for Mickey above the doors.
2 points

★ Look around **Mickey's Mainsail** shop

Clue 47: Peer at the exterior windows of the shop for Mickey.
3 points

Clue 48: Scan a rear window inside the shop for Mickey.
2 points

Clue 49: Look for Mickey in the designs on the Mainsail's walls, merchandise stands, and sales counters.
2 points

Clue 50: Gaze up for Mickey.
2 points

★ Go across the hall to the **Sea Treasures** shop.

Clue 51: Find Mickey in the shop design.
2 points

★ Stop by the Guest Services counter, **Deck 3 midship**.

Clue 52: Study the Atlantic Ocean map on the rear wall for a Hidden Mickey.
5 points

Clue 53: Switch to the Pacific Ocean map for another Hidden Mickey.
5 points

★ Take note of the **Bon Voyage** bar, Deck 3 midship.

Clue 54: Squint at the rear wall.
5 points

★ Stroll to the huge **atrium**, Deck 3 midship.

Clue 55: Glance around the atrium for outlines of Disney characters.
2 points

Clue 56: Look for more Disney characters in relief.
2 points

Clue 57: Search the scrollwork over the elevator shafts for classic Mickeys.
4 points for two or more

Clue 58: Study the railings that face the atrium.
3 points

Clue 59: Examine the sliding glass doors in the atrium lobby.
3 points for two Hidden Mickeys

★ Walk **aft to Animator's Palate** restaurant. (You can always enter at your assigned mealtime). Be sure to be courteous to the servers and other guests.

Clue 60: Study the mural just inside the entrance.
3 points

Clue 61: Glance down at the tile.
2 points

Clue 62: Admire the carpet inside the restaurant.
1 point

Clue 63: Don't miss the breadbasket and dishes!
3 points for both

Clue 64: Check out your server's clothing.
2 points

★ Walk down to **Deck 2 midship**.

Clue 65: Approach the Enchanted Garden restaurant and spot Hidden Mickeys.
3 points for all

★ **Ship restrooms**

Clue 66: Glance inside ship restrooms for Hidden Mickeys.
1 point for all

★ Check out **your stateroom** for Hidden Mickeys. (Mickey images can be found in many objects in the staterooms.)

Clue 67: Study various knobs.
2 points

Clue 68: Admire light fixtures.
2 points

Clue 69: Look in the bathroom.
2 points

★ **Remy** restaurant bonus points opportunity

Clue 70: If you go to Remy, look around for several Hidden Remys!
5 bonus points for images in five different places

Total Points for
the Disney Fantasy =

How'd you do?
Up to 80 points - Bronze
81 to 160 points - Silver
161 points and over - Gold
201 points - Perfect Score

(You may have done even better if you earned bonus points for Hidden Mickeys you found in your stateroom and Remy restaurant.)

Notes

Psst!

• • • • • • • • • • • • •

**Caution:
Don't peek at this
section unless you
really want help!**

• • • • • • • • • • • • •

Deck 5 midship

- Detective Game Registration Desk

Hint 1: During registration for the Midship Detective Agency game, a desktop with objects on it appears on the computer screen. A classic Mickey made of gears is drawn on the right side of a page on the desk entitled "For Review & Comment."

Hint 2: A small gold key on the right upper desktop area has Mickey ears.

Hint 3: A tiny, light blue full-body Mickey Mouse is at the top of the first note of a pad of white sticky notes on the right side of the desktop.

Deck 13 aft

HINTS HINTS HINTS HINTS HINTS HINTS HINTS HINTS HINTS HINTS HINTS HINTS HINTS

- Goofy's Sports Deck

Hint 4: Light blue classic Mickeys are on patches on Goofy's green golf bags at the beginning and end of Goofy Golf.

Hint 5: Classic Mickeys are inside Max's footprints along the golf course.

Hint 6: A classic Mickey made of white swirls hides in a blue coffee cup at the end of the ninth hole of Goofy Golf.

Hint 7: Large white classic Mickeys adorn the upper part of the support structure for the net that encloses the basketball court on Goofy's Sports Deck.

Deck 12 aft

- Meridian Lounge area

Hint 8: On the front of the huge, lighted circular map on the wall behind the receptionist counter for Palo and Remy restaurants, a classic Mickey impression lies in the middle circle of the metal star.

Hint 9: A classic Mickey impression is also in the middle circle of the metal star on the large, round light fixture hanging from the ceiling in the center of the Meridian Lounge.

Deck 12 midship

Hint 10: Visible from Deck 12 near midship, a colorful three-quarter profile of Mickey Mouse's face is on the bottom of Mickey's (children's) Pool. His big hand supports a water slide.

Hint 11: Donald Duck crashes headfirst into the port side of the ship's funnel midship. You can see his legs, rump, and life preserver. Hope he's okay!

Deck 13 forward funnel

- Edge

Hint 12: Classic Mickeys are scattered over the wallpaper inside the club.

Hint 13: Classic Mickeys appear inside some of the circles in both the turquoise and red carpets inside Edge.

Deck 11 forward

Hint 14: A tiny blue side-profile Mickey Mouse represents Mickey's Pool in the ship map on the wall by the Deck 11 elevators.

Hint 15: On some of the decks, guest room doorbells are surrounded by silver metal classic Mickeys.

Hint 16: Red classic Mickeys lie in the corners of some of the guest hallway carpet designs.

Deck 11 midship

Hint 17: The hour and minute hands of the clocks hanging on the Deck 12 railings above Mickey's and Donald's Pools are Mickey's own gloved hands.

- Nemo's Reef

Hint 18: Two classic Mickeys made of three white circles hide on the floor of Nemo's Reef. One is near a yellow fish and the other, near a blowfish. Some other circles on the floor here come close to forming classic Hidden Mickeys but don't meet all the criteria (see *Chapter One*).

Hint 19: A faint white classic Mickey is painted on the top of the upper crossbar of Mr. Ray's water slide.

Deck 11 aft

- Cabanas restaurant

Hint 20: The frames supporting the wooden benches with padded seats have classic Mickey holes in the front. Psst! They're right behind your legs.

Hint 21: Near the bottom of the window posts, silver classic Mickeys secure the chains of the window coverings inside the restaurant.

Hint 22: Subtle classic Mickeys are scattered over drinking glasses.

Deck 10 forward

Hint 23: A silver classic Mickey lies on a silver strip under the elevator doors.

Hint 24: On the wall near the Deck 10 forward elevators, a pink octopus appears at one point in an interactive painting with Ariel. A classic Mickey formed of bumps is on the upper right of the octopus's head.

Stairwell between
Decks 7 and 6 forward

Hint 25: Silver bumps at the lower right-hand side of a picture frame on the stairwell wall form a classic Mickey. Similar images in the frame resemble classic Mickeys but are less convincing.

Deck 5 forward

- Buena Vista Theatre

Hint 26: Blue classic Mickeys are in the hallway carpet outside the theatre. (This carpet design also appears inside the theatre.)

Hint 27: Light brown classic Mickey "hats" (classic Mickeys with the "head" circle cut in half) lie low on the hallway wall outside the theatre.

Hint 28: Inside the theatre, the ornamental scroll-work design on light fixtures along the side walls includes classic Mickeys.

Hint 29: Classic Mickeys ring the small central part of the huge star-shaped light fixture hanging from the center of the theatre ceiling.

Hint 30: Small white classic Mickeys are repeated in the pattern of the theatre seats.

Deck 5 midship

Hint 31: In an interactive map of the Caribbean Sea on a wall at Deck 5 midship, a red classic Mickey sits on Castaway Cay and a black classic Mickey is in the middle of the compass at the lower left of the map.

Hint 32: Small classic Mickeys are near the top of the multicolored atrium chandelier.

- Disney's Oceaneer Club

Hint 33: Inside the Oceaneer Club, Tinker Bell and other characters are traced in points of light on the ceiling.

Hint 34: In the Club's Andy's Room, a full-body Mickey rests on the face of a green watch that's hanging on the right wall.

Hint 35: White classic Mickeys move in and out on the digital Activities Board on the wall in front of the Club. (You can spot similar white classic Mickeys on Activities Boards for other clubs around the ship.)

- Disney's Oceaneer Lab

Hint 36: On the shelf in the far left display window behind the entrance gates, three gold coins in front of a chest form a classic Mickey.

Deck 5 aft

Hint 37: As your detective card activates the game in the interactive painting near the aft elevators, a classic Mickey made of orange gears appears as the game begins.

Hint 38: As the game progresses, a tiny upside-down classic Mickey appears. It's in the frame with the newspaper at the top with the headline, "Fur Flies In … ." Look for this Hidden Mickey as you move your magnifying glass around the painting. It will appear under your magnifying glass at the lower right of the painting to the left of the words "Cove Cafe."

Deck 4 aft

- Skyline Lounge

Hint 39: A full-figure Mickey Mouse walks across an open window on an upper floor of a building in the dynamic scene of London on the rear wall of the lounge. (You may also spot some *Star Wars* characters walking across open windows on the floor directly below Mickey.)

Deck 4 midship

- D Lounge

Hint 40: Some of the large circular light fixtures on the ceiling of D Lounge form classic Mickeys.

Hint 41: Several sections of the carpet have circles of brown, black, or white. Some groups of circles form classic Mickeys with light brown Mickey "heads."

- Shutters

Hint 42: Classic Mickeys are hidden in the design of the ornamental scrollwork on the photo shop's sales counter and on some of its cabinets. (You'll also find decorative Mickey images scattered around the shop.)

Decks 4 and 3 forward

- Walt Disney Theatre

Hint 43: Inside the theatre, classic Mickeys are in the ornamental detail above, along the front, and at the side of the stage.

Hint 44: Also inside, classic Mickeys are repeated in the ornamental design under the railings and above the balcony.

Hint 45: Classic Mickeys hide in the red fabric that covers the theatre's large speakers. One is at the upper left and another, smaller classic Mickey is at the upper right of the fabric.

Deck 3 forward

- Elevators

Hint 46: Above some of the elevator doors (such as the Deck 3 forward elevators), Mickey's hand points to the deck level.

- Mickey's Mainsail shop

Hint 47: A small side-profile Mickey sits in a boat under the "M" of "MainSail" in the shop logo that is painted in white on the hall windows along the outer wall of the shop.

Hint 48: At the rear of Mickey's Mainsail, small classic Mickeys are in the round perimeters of the porthole windows.

Hint 49: Mickey hats, with incomplete swirls for ears, hide in the design of the friezes high on the shop's walls, at the top of some merchandise stands, and on the front of the sales counter.

Hint 50: White classic Mickeys hide along the side and at the bottom of the circular ceiling chandelier inside Mickey's Mainsail.

- Sea Treasures shop

Hint 51: The friezes high up on the shop's walls near the ceiling hide classic Mickeys in their design and classic Mickeys can also be found atop some of Sea Treasures' merchandise stands.

Deck 3 midship

- Guest Services

Hint 52: On the wall behind the Guest Services counter, find the map with the Atlantic Ocean. A faint, white partial classic Mickey lies to the left of the Tokyo Disneyland Castle in Asia.

Hint 53: Move over to the rear wall map with the Pacific Ocean. A faint, white classic Mickey hides below the words "North America."

- Bon Voyage Bar

Hint 54: In the rear wall art, find a classic Hidden Mickey in the outer "eye" (near the outer edge) of the peacock feathers.

- Atrium

Hint 55: Disney characters (Donald, Goofy, and so on) are repeated in the design of the atrium's staircase railings outside the Royal Court restaurant.

Hint 56: Disney characters are also featured in relief on the gold horizontal friezes on the edges of the walkways around the atrium on Decks 4 and 5. You can see them well when standing in front of Royal Court restaurant.

Hint 57: Classic Mickeys appear in various areas of the scrollwork adorning the elevator shafts facing the atrium lobby.

Hint 58: The design at the bottom of the deck railings facing the atrium also harbor classic Mickeys.

54

Hint 59: Classic Mickeys hide in the design etched on the sliding glass doors at the side of the atrium lobby. These doors are open when guests are boarding and disembarking the ship.

Deck 3 aft

- Animator's Palate

Hint 60: On the mural just inside the entrance to the restaurant, a running and jumping Dalmatian dog with black spots on its right upper leg appears in a series of drawings. In some of the drawings, the black spots form classic Mickeys.

Hint 61: Also just inside the entrance, white classic Mickeys are sprinkled around the large circle of dark floor tile.

Hint 62: Classic Mickeys hide in the carpet inside the restaurant.

Hint 63: Some of the circles in the wire breadbasket form classic Mickeys, and classic Mickeys also decorate the right side of the dishes.

Hint 64: Animator's Palate servers sport classic Mickey belt buckles!

Deck 2 midship

- Enchanted Garden

Hint 65: The ornamental metalwork of the entrance gate to the restaurant shelters classic Mickeys.

Ship Restrooms

Hint 66: In many of the ship's restrooms, the large round mirrors are topped with round lights or smaller round mirrors that together form classic Mickeys above some of the restroom sinks.

In your stateroom

Hint 67: Classic Mickeys hide in the middle of the metal knobs on your stateroom desk.

Hint 68: Classic Mickey holes decorate the metal bands around various lamps and light fixtures.

Hint 69: A rope design in the shower curtain forms classic Mickeys. (Similar rope-design classic Mickeys hide on the rolling housekeeping bags in the guest hallways.)

Remy restaurant

Hint 70: Images of Remy are scattered around the restaurant. They're in the fabric of the dining booths, in a gold strip on the walls, in the woodwork of a mirror, and in woodwork on the back of chairs. A full-body glass Remy hides atop a lighting fixture.

CHAPTER 4

Disney Magic®
Scavenger Hunt

•••••••••••••••••••••••••••••

Note: This Hunt includes only those places that harbor confirmed Hidden Mickeys. So if the area you're looking in isn't included, Mickey isn't hiding there. Or if he is, I haven't yet spotted him.

★ Before you start, go to Guest Services on **Deck 3 midship** and find out when "Open House" is scheduled for Disney's Oceaneer Club (for ages 3 to 7) and Vibe (for teens). Plan your visits accordingly. (You can enter anytime if you have a child registered in the club.)

★ Walk to the Wide World of Sports area on **Deck 10 forward**.

Clue 1: Look for Mickey in front of and below you.
2 points

Clue 2: Search for Mickey over your head.
3 points

★ Stroll back to the midship area and take the stairs (or the elevator) to **Deck 11**.

Clue 3: Find Mickey inside *Vibe*.
2 points

★ Return to **Deck 10** and walk **aft**.

Clue 4: Gaze at a big Mickey's profile.
2 points

★ Go below to **Deck 9 aft**.

Clue 5: Spot poles with Mickey holes and supports.
2 points

★ Now descend to **Deck 6 midship**.

Clue 6: Find a mural with six different Hidden Character images.
10 points for all six

★ Go below to **Deck 5 aft**.

Clue 7: Look around inside the Buena Vista Theatre for some Hidden Mickeys.
3 points

Clue 8: Search for a tiny, white classic Mickey in the hall nearby.
4 points

Clue 9: If the Cast Members allow you in, find two Hidden Mickeys inside Flounder's Reef Nursery.
4 bonus points

★ Walk forward into **Disney's Oceaneer Club**.

Clue 10: Look around to spot Mickey's hands.
2 points

Clue 11: Then look up for Mickey in lights!
5 points

★ Now **exit** the Club **and walk forward**. On the way …

Clue 12: Find five Hidden Characters on the wall. (A sixth image is too obvious—not hidden).
20 points for all five

★ Go to the **Deck 5 forward stairs**.

Clue 13: Don't miss two Disney characters hiding in the stairwell!
5 points for both

★ Go below to **Deck 4 forward**.

Clue 14: When you can look inside the Walt Disney Theatre, don't miss classic Mickeys around you!
3 points

Clue 15: Inside Mickey's Mates, poke around to spot a classic Mickey.
3 points

Clue 16: Study the display windows of the Treasure Ketch shop for a brown Hidden Mickey.
3 points

Clue 17: In another Treasure Ketch display window admire a tiny gold Hidden Mickey.
5 points

★ Walk to the **Deck 4 midship stairs**.

Clue 18: Find six Hidden Characters in the stairwell.
8 points for all

★ Walk aft on Deck 4 port side and stroll through **Shutters**.

Clue 19: Admire a classic Mickey in a photo.
4 points

★ Step outside onto the **Promenade** and look aft.

Clue 20: Study the struts overhead for some Hidden Mickeys.
5 points for one or more

★ Enter **Animator's Palate**.

Clue 21: Gaze at the walls inside the restaurant for a Hidden Mickey repeated three times.
4 points for spotting all three

★ Study the **elevator lobby** next.

Clue 22: Spot Mickey outside the elevators. (Psst! He's in the same spots on Deck 3.)
2 points for one or more

★ Go below to **Deck 3** and walk forward to the **lobby atrium**.

Clue 23: Admire the elevators across from Lumiere's restaurant. (Mickey is there!)
5 points for two

Clue 24: Now look up between the elevators for another Hidden Mickey.
4 points

Clue 25: Glance around the atrium for outlines of a number of Disney characters.
2 points

Clue 26: Look up high for more Disney characters.
2 points

Clue 27: Keep looking up overhead for some classic Mickeys.
3 points

Clue 28: Now search for at least six Hidden Characters in an atrium display.
15 points for all

Clue 29: Find a Disney character near the Shore Excursions counter.
5 points

Clue 30: Now check for Mickey in the Guest Services area.
4 points

★ Stroll forward to the **Rockin' Bar D**.

Clue 31: Mickey is hiding inside near the floor!
3 points

Clue 32: Now look up in the bar area to find another Mickey image.
3 points

★ Don't forget to search **your stateroom**.

Clue 33: Find Hidden Mickeys on your stateroom lamps.
2 points

Give yourself bonus points for any other Hidden Mickeys you find inside your stateroom.
1 bonus point for each Mickey you spot

Note: Stateroom Hidden Mickeys may change over time.

Done looking? Then it's time to tally your score.

Total Points for
the Disney Magic =

How'd you do?
Up to 60 points - Bronze
61 to 118 points - Silver
119 points and over - Gold
149 points - Perfect Score

(You may have done even better if you earned bonus points spotting Hidden Mickeys in your stateroom or inside Flounder's Reef Nursery.)

Notes

**Caution:
Don't peek at this
section unless you
really want help!**

Deck 10

- Wide World of Sports area

Hint 1: A classic Mickey is cut out on the bow of the *Disney Magic* where the flags are hoisted when the ship leaves or sails into a port. (The holes are often covered, but you can easily see the Mickey image even with the cover in place.)

Hint 2: Along the outer walkway, an overhead brace has holes that are proportioned correctly to be a classic Mickey.

Deck 11 midship

- Vibe

Hint 3: A classic Mickey is on a wall above an inside door.

Deck 10 aft

Hint 4: Visible from Deck 10 aft, a colorful three-quarter profile of Mickey Mouse's face is on the bottom of Mickey's (children's) Pool. His big hand holds up a water slide.

Deck 9

Hint 5: Poles to hold merchandise are often found around Deck 9. They have Mickey-shaped holes and bottom supports.

Deck 6 midship

Hint 6: Go behind the elevators on Deck 6 midship for the best view of six Hidden Character images on a mural. Donald Duck's uniform is draped over the railing above the man reading the newspaper. On the newspaper, look for a black classic Mickey, three different fish classic Mickeys (the scales, the eye, and the nearby bubbles) and Minnie Mouse's shoes.

Deck 5 aft

- Buena Vista Theatre

Hint 7: Inside the Buena Vista Theatre, classic Mickey designs are on the side walls of the auditorium and the borders of the stage.

- Flounder's Reef Nursery

Hint 8: Look closely at the bubbles in the Flounder's Reef Nursery sign outside the nursery. You'll find a tiny white classic Mickey in the bubbles. It's near the letter "f" of "Reef."

Hint 9: If the Cast Members allow you to step inside the nursery, look for two more bubble classic Mickeys, one on the left wall mural and another toward the rear of the nursery on the right wall.

Deck 5 midship

- Disney's Oceaneer Club

Hint 10: Inside Disney's Oceaneer Club, Deck 5 midship, Mickey's gloved hands cover a ship's wheel upstairs and to the right.

Hint 11: On the ceiling of Disney's Oceaneer Club, Sorcerer Mickey is outlined in points of light above the middle of the floor.

- Hallway wall forward of the Club

Hint 12: Ten pictures grace a hallway wall on the port side of the ship between the midship and forward elevators (the wall to your right as you face forward). As you face the wall, Donald Duck hides on a utensil in the eighth picture from the left. Mickey hides on pillows in the sixth picture. "Steamboat Willie" Mickey is pictured on a pail in the third picture, and Goofy and Dopey stand in a coffee queue in the first picture on the left.

Note: You can also see Mickey driving a car in one of the photos. But he's too obvious to be considered hidden.

Deck 5 to 4 forward stairs

Hint 13: Halfway down the forward stairs from Deck 5 to Deck 4, a picture on the wall to the right has an image of Goofy snorkeling, and a picture on the wall to the left shows Snow White dancing.

Deck 4 forward

- Walt Disney Theatre

Hint 14: Inside the Walt Disney Theatre, classic Mickeys are mixed in with the decorative designs on the wall.

- Mickey's Mates

Hint 15: Just inside the hallway entrance to the Mickey's Mates store, Goofy holds a rope that's looped to form a classic Mickey. (The image may be distorted from time to time, since probing hands can reach it.)

- Treasure Ketch

Hint 16: In a display window of the Treasure Ketch shop, a classic Mickey is on the U.S.A. map in the position of Disneyland.

Hint 17: In a display window to the right of the entrance (from the main hallway) to the shop, look closely at "Disco Mickey." He sports a gold chain necklace with a classic Mickey in the center.

Deck 4 to 3 midship stairwell

Hint 18: A circular "star map" is mounted in the stairwell between Decks 3 and 4 midship. The "map" includes constellations that form profiles of Mickey and Donald. Along with the Mickey and Donald constellations, look for drawings of Pluto and Donald's nephews in the picture.

Deck 4 midship

- Shutters

Hint 19: On a wall inside Shutters, a photo shows the classic Mickey-shaped sand trap at the sixth green of the Magnolia Golf Course at Walt Disney World® Resort.

Deck 4 aft

- On the Promenade outside Animator's Palate

Hint 20: Above Deck 4 outside Animator's Palate restaurant, several groups of bolts on stanchions for the lifeboats form classic Mickeys.

- Inside Animator's Palate

Hint 21: Inside the Animator's Palate Restaurant, a classic Mickey is repeated on a cup halfway along the right wall (as you enter the restaurant), on the right side of the right rear wall, and in the middle of the left rear wall.

- Elevator doors

Hint 22: On both Decks 4 and 3, Mickey's hand appears above every elevator door, his finger pointing to the different floors.

Deck 3 midship

- Outside Lumiere's

Hint 23: The scrollwork on the elevators across from Lumiere's restaurant has Mickey hats in the design, and upside-down classic Mickeys at the bottom right of some elevators.

Hint 24: Between the elevators across from Lumiere's, three silver circles on the bottom of a light brown design on the wall form a classic Mickey.

Hint 25: Outside Lumiere's, Disney characters are repeated in the design of the staircase railings.

- Atrium lobby

Hint 26: Check out the atrium balconies. Character images are embossed in the decorative metal bands around the bottoms of the balconies. The same characters appear in the horizontal friezes around the main lobby in front of Lumiere's restaurant.

Hint 27: Stand near the elevators and look up at the atrium chandelier. You can spot one or more classic Mickeys in the chandelier.

Hint 28: In a picture window display near the Shore Excursions counter, focus on the model building that looks a bit like a ship.

It's decorated with character statues (Peter Pan, Captain Hook, and Winnie the Pooh, among others) as well as friezes and pillars. You'll find Tinker Bell and classic Mickeys in the horizontal friezes along the building walls. Classic Mickeys adorn the awning on the right and the fan vaulting above a door on the left. A side-profile Mickey hides at the top of the street lamp, Mickey T-shirts are featured in the building's bottom right windows, and Mickey himself is high up in the crow's-nest.

Hint 29: On the right side of a mural behind the Shore Excursions counter, Donald Duck hides on a pail that's sitting on the sand by a palm tree.

Hint 30: Mickey lies under a beach umbrella (his shorts and legs are visible) on the mural behind the Guest Services counter.

Deck 3 forward

- *Rockin' Bar D*

Hint 31: The footrests on the bar stools in Rockin' Bar D form Classic Mickeys.

Hint 32: On a silver radio on an upper shelf above the bar at the rear of the Rockin' Bar D, the speaker holes form classic Mickeys.

In your stateroom

Hint 33: Inside the staterooms, classic Mickeys are repeated along the bottoms of lampshades.

Disney Wonder® Scavenger Hunt

• •

Note: This Hunt includes only those places that harbor confirmed Hidden Mickeys. So if the area you're looking in isn't included, Mickey isn't hiding there. Or if he is, I haven't yet spotted him.

★ Before you start, go to Guest Services on **Deck 3 midship** and find out when "Open House" is scheduled for Disney's Oceaneer Club (for ages 3 to 7) and Vibe (for teens), and plan your visits accordingly. You can also enter anytime if you have a child registered in the club.

★ Walk to the Wide World of Sports area on **Deck 10 forward**.

Clue 1: Look for Mickey in front of and below you.
2 points

Clue 2: Search for Mickey over your head.
3 points

★ Stroll back to the midship area and take the stairs or elevator to **Deck 11**.

Clue 3: Find Mickey inside Vibe.
2 points

★ Return to **Deck 10** midship and walk aft.

Clue 4: Gaze down at a big Mickey profile.
2 points

★ Go below to **Deck 9 aft**.

Clue 5: Spot poles with Mickey holes and supports.
2 points

Clue 6: Walk inside Beach Blanket Buffet and study the floor.
5 points

★ Descend to **Deck 5 aft**.

Clue 7: Look around inside the Buena Vista Theatre for some Hidden Mickeys.
3 points

Clue 8: Search for a tiny, white classic Mickey in the hall nearby.
4 points

★ Now head into **Disney's Oceaneer Club**.

Clue 9: Inside Disney's Oceaneer Club, spot Mickey's hands.
2 points

Clue 10: Keep your eyes up for Tinker Bell.
5 points

Clue 11: Search for a classic Mickey on a box.
4 points

Clue 12: Find a classic Mickey near the restrooms in the rear of Disney's Oceaneer Club.
4 points

★ Walk to **Deck 5 forward**.

Clue 13: On the wall, spot Mickey by a ship's wheel.
3 points

Clue 14: On the wall, look for Mickey going fast.
4 points

★ Go below to **Deck 4 forward**.

Clue 15: When you can look inside the Walt Disney Theatre, don't miss classic Mickeys around you!
3 points

Clue 16: Poke around inside Mickey's Mates to spot a classic Mickey.
3 points

★ Stroll aft to **Studio Sea**.

Clue 17: Search outside Studio Sea for a Hidden Mickey.
3 points

★ Continue walking aft and stroll through **Shutters**.

Clue 18: Admire a classic Mickey in a photo.
4 points

★ Step outside onto the **Promenade** and look around.

Clue 19: Study the struts overhead carefully for a Hidden Mickey.
5 points

★ Step back inside and stare at the walls outside of **Animator's Palate**.

Clue 20: Can you spot a classic Mickey?
3 points

★ Enter Animator's Palate.

Clue 21: Inside the restaurant, Mickey is hiding on the wall.
3 points

★ Now check out the **elevator lobby**.

Clue 22: On Decks 4 or 3 (or both), spot Mickey outside the elevators.
2 points for one or more

★ Go below to **Deck 3 aft** if you haven't already done so.

Clue 23: Study the walls nearby for Hidden Mickeys.
3 points

★ Head forward and wander around **Triton's restaurant**.

Clue 24: Search the outside of the restaurant for Hidden Mickeys.
3 points

Clue 25: Now look inside Triton's for two very large Hidden Mickeys.
3 points

★ Outside the restaurant in the **lobby atrium**, Deck 3 midship …

Clue 26: Admire the nearby elevators. Psst! Mickey is there!
3 points

Clue 27: Search up between the elevators for a classic Mickey.
3 points

Clue 28: Now glance around the atrium for outlines of Disney characters.
2 points

Clue 29: Look up high for more Disney characters.
2 points

Clue 30: Keep looking up overhead for some classic Mickeys.
3 points

Clue 31: Search for Mickey's hands nearby.
4 points

Clue 32: Don't miss some nearby Disney characters. They're in a display!
3 points

Clue 33: Walk to a nearby mural and spot a Hidden Mickey.
4 points

Clue 34: Look down for some Hidden Mickeys below a counter.
3 points

Clue 35: Search for Mickey in another mural.
2 points

Clue 36: Now look down for Hidden Mickeys below another counter.
3 points

★ Walk to **Deck 3 forward**.

Clue 37: Spot some Hidden Mickeys right in front of WaveBands.
3 points

Clue 38: Search for a large Hidden Mickey inside WaveBands.
4 points

Clue 39: Find a small Hidden Mickey on WaveBands' floor.
5 points

★ Stroll over to **Cadillac Lounge**.

Clue 40: Look around for Mickey on a wall.
5 points

★ Now walk to the **Deck 3 forward stairs**.

Clue 41: Donald Duck is hiding nearby.
4 points

Clue 42: Spot Pluto, too!
4 points

★ Enjoy the **deck parties**!

Clue 43: Watch Mickey as he zooms by overhead between the ship's funnels. Can you spot a Hidden Mickey nearby?
5 points

★ Inside **your stateroom** ...

Clue 44: Find some classic Mickeys on your stateroom lamps.
2 points

Give yourself bonus points for any other Hidden Mickeys you find in your stateroom.
1 bonus point for each Mickey you spot

Note: The Hidden Mickey images in staterooms may change over time.

It's time to total your score!

Total Points for
the Disney Wonder =

```
┌─────────────────────┐
│                     │
│                     │
│                     │
└─────────────────────┘
```

How'd you do?
Up to 58 points - Bronze
59 to 114 points - Silver
115 points and over - Gold
144 points - Perfect Score

(If you earned bonus points for Hidden Mickeys you found in your stateroom, you may have done even better!)

**Caution:
Don't peek at this
section unless you
really want help!**

Deck 10 forward

- *Wide World of Sports area*

Hint 1: Visible from the Wide World of Sports area on Deck 10 forward, a large classic Mickey is cut out of the bow of the ship. (These holes are often covered, but the Mickey image is easily visible even with the covers in place).

Hint 2: Along the outer walkway, some of the overhead braces have holes that are proportioned correctly to be classic Mickeys.

Deck 11 midship

- *Vibe lounge*

Hint 3: A classic Mickey is on a wall above a door inside this teen activity center.

Deck 10 aft

Hint 4: Visible from Deck 10 aft, a colorful three-quarter profile of Mickey Mouse's face is on the bottom of Mickey's (children's) Pool on Deck 9. His big hand holds up a water slide.

Deck 9 aft

Hint 5: Poles to hold merchandise are often found around Deck 9. They have Mickey-shaped holes and bottom supports.

Hint 6: Inside Beach Blanket Buffet, a "worn" area on the floor forms a classic Mickey. Look down to the right just past the end of the serving line on the right-hand side (as seen when facing the serving area) to find him.

Deck 5 aft

- Buena Vista Theatre

Hint 7: Inside the Buena Vista Theatre, classic Mickey designs can be found in the side walls of the auditorium and the borders of the stage.

- Outside Flounder's Reef Nursery

Hint 8: A tiny white classic Mickey hides in the bubbles in the Flounder's Reef Nursery sign outside, near the letter "f" of "Reef."

Deck 5 midship

- Disney's Oceaneer Club

Hint 9: Inside Disney's Oceaneer Club, Mickey's gloved hands cover a ship's wheel. You'll find it upstairs and to the right.

Hint 10: Near Sorcerer Mickey, Tinker Bell is outlined in green points of light.

Hint 11: In a stack of boxes on the floor, you

can spot a black classic Mickey smudge on top of the second red box from the floor.

Hint 12: Near the Club's restrooms, you'll find a small, dark classic Mickey spot on the wall to the left of a drinking fountain.

Deck 5 forward

Hint 13: Walk to the nearby portside hall to look at photos of the *Disney Wonder* on the wall. In one of the photos (near the end on the right), you can spot a full figure painting of Mickey Mouse standing at a ship's wheel.

Hint 14: In the same photo, you'll find another painting of Mickey—this time in side profile driving a jet ski.

Deck 4 forward

- Walt Disney Theatre

Hint 15: Inside the Walt Disney Theatre, classic Mickeys are mixed in with the decorative designs on the wall.

- Mickey's Mates

Hint 16: Just inside the hall entrance to the Mickey's Mates store, Goofy holds a rope looped to form a classic Mickey. (The image may be distorted from time to time, since probing hands can reach it.)

Deck 4 midship

- Studio Sea

Hint 17: The small silver discs on the rear doors of Studio Sea sport classic Mickeys.

- Shutters

Hint 18: On a wall inside Shutters, a photo shows the classic Mickey-shaped sand trap at the sixth green of the Magnolia Golf Course at Walt Disney World® Resort.

Deck 4 aft

- Outside on the Promenade

Hint 19: Above the Deck 4 Promenade outside of Animator's Palate restaurant, three bolts on a stanchion for the lifeboats form a classic Mickey.

- Indoors, outside Animator's Palate

Hint 20: Along the inside hall that leads to and from Animator's Palate restaurant, a black classic Mickey is at the upper left of a picture frame on the wall.

- Inside Animator's Palate

Hint 21: You can spot a classic Mickey on the left wall just inside the restaurant's main entrance.

- Elevator lobbies

Hint 22: On Decks 3 and 4, Mickey's hand is above every elevator door pointing to the numbers for the different floors.

Deck 3 aft

Hint 23: In a painting outside Parrot Cay restaurant on Deck 3 aft, you can spot classic Mickeys on the smokestacks of Disney cruise ships. Check the wall near the stairs.

Deck 3 midship

- Triton's restaurant

Hint 24: Classic Mickeys are in the restaurant's outer glass wall.

Hint 25: There are two gigantic classic Mickeys on Triton's ceiling. They are best viewed from either the port or starboard wall of the restaurant.

- Atrium lobby

Hint 26: The metal scrollwork near the atrium elevators across from Triton's includes classic Mickey hats.

Hint 27: On the wall between the elevators across from Triton's main entrance, scan the light brown design above your head to find a gold classic Mickey on the bottom of the design.

Hint 28: Disney characters (Minnie, Goofy, etc.) are repeated in the design of the staircase railings outside Triton's restaurant.

Hint 29: Disney characters are also in the relief design of the horizontal friezes around the area in front of Triton's restaurant.

Hint 30: Viewed from near the elevators (your best vantage point), the atrium chandelier above you includes some classic Mickeys.

Hint 31: Mickey Mouse's hands appear twice in a corner wall display outside Triton's restaurant.

Hint 32: Classic characters are in a window wall display near the atrium.

Hint 33: The mural behind the Shore Excursions counter includes a classic Mickey.

Hint 34: The front of the Shore Excursions counter is decorated with some classic tri-circle Hidden Mickeys.

Hint 35: You'll find a classic Mickey on top of the "Nassau" sign in the mural behind the Guest Services counter (on the other side of the elevators from the Shore Excursions counter).

Hint 36: The front of this Guest Services counter has classic Mickey circles at the far left and right.

Deck 3 forward

- WaveBands

Hint 37: Records on the floor in front of and inside WaveBands form classic Mickeys.

Hint 38: The WaveBands dance floor is shaped like a classic Mickey, but it's half-covered by the stage.

Hint 39: On the floor near the stage, a blue classic Mickey is formed in smoke from a smokestack.

- Cadillac Lounge

Hint 40: Inside Cadillac Lounge, check out the front wall mural. You can find classic Mickey lights in the lower middle section of the mural, below the tallest building.

- forward stairway

Hint 41: In a painting on the wall halfway up the Deck 3 forward stairs, you'll find the figure of Donald Duck on a car.

Hint 42: Pluto is on a car in another painting on this same wall.

Aloft between the ship's funnels

Hint 43: A classic Mickey rides high aloft in a silver metal "trolley" that runs between the ship's funnels during special deck parties carrying Mickey Mouse himself. The Main Mouse (a decorative Mickey) hangs from the trolley. You can see him and the classic Mickey from Decks 9 and 10.

In your stateroom

Hint 44: Inside the staterooms, classic Mickeys are repeated along the bottoms of lampshades.

CHAPTER 6

Castaway Cay Scavenger Hunt

•••••••••••••••••••••••••••••

★ Walk a ways **past the end of the gangway** and look around.

Clue 1: Spot one or more Hidden Disney characters as you exit your ship onto Castaway Cay.
4 points

★ As you continue **on the walkway** toward the island proper ...

Clue 2: Check out some swinging doors.
2 points

Clue 3: Stay alert for some coconuts.
5 points

★ Along the **path to the beaches** ...

Clue 4: Look around for a part of Mickey.
3 points

★ **Across from the First Aid Cabin** as you approach the first shops and beaches ...

Clue 5: Mickey and friends are smiling at you!
2 points

★ In the **shops and eateries area** ...

Clue 6: Look up in one of the nearby seating areas to find Mickey.
4 points

★ Now take a close look **inside** the **Conched Out Bar**.

Clue 7: Search around inside the bar for two classic Mickeys.
10 points for both

Clue 8: Now see if you can spot where Mickey Mouse is standing inside the bar.
5 points

★ Head to **In-Da-Shade Game Pavilion**.

Clue 9: Keep your eyes open for a Hidden Mickey.
5 points

★ Walk to the **Pelican Plunge observation area**.

Clue 10: Look at the water slide. Can you see Mickey?
3 points

Clue 11: Search the water in front of you for a Hidden Mickey.
5 points

★ Amble over to **Cookie's Too BBQ**

Clue 12: Study the shelves inside for a classic Mickey.
4 points

Note: It's a long walk to the Observation Tower and to Serenity Bay Beach and back. You may want to grab a bicycle at the rental area that's located on the way to the airstrip.

★ As you stroll or bike **toward Serenity Bay Beach** ...

Clue 13: Look for a flying Disney character that you'll pass on the way.
4 points

★ Take the path on your right and go to the **Observation Tower**.

Clue 14: Climb the Observation Tower to the 2nd or 3rd level and study the landscape nearby for two Hidden Mickeys.
10 points for spotting both

★ Resume your trek **to Serenity Bay Beach**.

Clue 15: Find a Disney character at the end of the old airstrip, very near the beach.
4 points

★ Walk near the **Castaway Air Bar** on Serenity Bay Beach.

Clue 16: Search in the trees for Jessica Rabbit.
5 points

★ Look for underwater Hidden Images in the **Snorkeling Lagoon**.

Clue 17: If you're up for some snorkeling, don't miss the two underwater statues of Mickey and Minnie!
10 points

Clue 18: Swim around to spot two classic Mickeys in cement balls on the bottom of the lagoon.
10 points for both

Now turn the page and total your score.

Total Points for
Castaway Cay =

How'd you do?
Up to 38 points - Bronze
39 to 75 points - Silver
76 points and over - Gold
95 points - Perfect Score

**Caution:
Don't peek at this
section unless you
really want help!**

As you disembark

Hint 1: You can see Disney characters playing around on the ship's stern when you look back at the ship soon after you disembark onto Castaway Cay.

On the walkway to the island proper

Hint 2: At the side of Marge's Barges & Sea Charters check-in cabin, the swinging doors to the dock have classic Mickey holes.

Hint 3: Just a short walk from the ship's gangway as you enter Castaway Cay, keep your eyes peeled for the photo spot across from where the first tram loads (the Kargo Handling Tram Stop). A classic Mickey is formed by three coconuts on the Coconut Lotion Barrel in the background of the photo backdrop.

HINTS HINTS HINTS HINTS HINTS HINTS HINTS HINTS HINTS HINTS HINTS HINTS

Path to beaches

Hint 4: As you travel along the path to the beaches, look to your right to see Mickey's hand showing you where the fun is! You'll find this image about halfway along on the right side as you walk (or ride the tram) to the first shops and beaches.

- Mount Rustmore photo spot

Hint 5: Check out Mickey Mouse and friends at a photo spot called Mount Rustmore. It's across from the First Aid cabin as you approach the first shops and beaches.

Shops and eateries area

- near Cookie's BBQ

Hint 6: A big, white fluffy classic Mickey hangs high in the rafters of one of the Dining Pavilions near Cookie's BBQ.

- Conched Out Bar

Hint 7: Two different sets of coins form classic Mickeys on the laminated counters of the bar. One set of gold coins is on the middle of the side counter of the bar's left side (as you face the bar from the main walkway). The other is on the right side of the front counter, under the bar sign and under the rightmost awning. This second set of coins is partially covered with sand.

Hint 8: A rusted image of Mickey stands on a high inside shelf above the Conched Out Bar's side counter. You can see it by looking to the upper left as you sit at the front counter (the counter facing the main walkway).

- In-Da-Shade Game Pavilion

Hint 9: A classic Mickey made of colorful bicycle wheels hangs inside the separate covered area on the left side of the In-Da-Shade Game Pavilion area.

- Pelican Plunge

Hint 10: Life preservers form a classic Mickey on the roof of the Pelican Plunge water slides.

Hint 11: Three black rocks in the shallow water near the Pelican Plunge observation deck form a classic Mickey. They are best seen from the far left of the observation deck.

- Cookie's Too BBQ

Hint 12: Walk to the right side of Cookie's Too BBQ and enter on the far right side of the serving area. Look across the building to a shelf on the wall opposite you for a classic Mickey made of plates. This Hidden Mickey is above a row of five plates on the wall.

On the way to Serenity Bay Beach

- "Castaway Air" plane

Hint 13: Donald Duck is on the "Castaway Air" plane that sits to your right, halfway down the old airstrip that takes you back to the Serenity Bay (adults-only) Beach.

- Observation Tower

Hint 14: Look for pelicans on the ground behind the Observation Tower. One pelican is standing in a bathtub and two pelicans nearby are on a bicycle. Both the bathtub and the bicycle appear to be powered by motorized fans. The bathtub fan has a black classic Mickey on its red motor housing, and the bicycle fan has a black classic Mickey on its orange motor housing.

- Airplane in bushes

Hint 15: At the far end of the old airstrip and close to Serenity Bay Beach, an airplane in the bushes sports a Donald Duck emblem.

Serenity Bay Beach

- *Castaway Air Bar*

Hint 16: An image of Jessica Rabbit is hidden in the trees above Castaway Air Bar. Go to the side of the bar with the restrooms and look above the "Daughters" sign (for the women's restroom). You have to move around in the general area to spot Jessica between tree branches above the roof of the bar. She's positioned to the left of, and on the same level as, the "Castaway Air Bar" sign.

Snorkeling Lagoon

Hint 17: A sunken Mickey statue stands at the left side of the lagoon, and a sunken Minnie statue stands toward the front of the lagoon near a lifeguard stand. (These statues may be moved around at times.)

Hint 18: On the bottom of the snorkeling lagoon, one cement ball has three holes that are close enough together to form a proportional Hidden Mickey. The second cement ball has a complete cutout of Mickey's head and ears. Both balls may be moved around at times, but the cutout Mickey ball is usually at the rear of the snorkeling lagoon near the border ropes.

CHAPTER 7

Other Mickey Appearances

These Hidden Mickeys won't earn you any points, but you're bound to enjoy them if you're in the right place at the right time to see them.

Look for holiday Hidden Mickeys on the ships and on Castaway Cay. These images may change from year to year.

Other Mickey images (decorative and deliberate) appear with some regularity on the ships and the island. You may find the Mickster on brochures, maps and flags, Cast Member nametags, stateroom keys, and restaurant and shop receipts. The restaurants sometimes offer classic Mickey butter and margarine pats, pancakes and waffles, and pizzas and pasta, as well as Mickey napkins. They also may arrange dishes and condiments to form classic Mickeys. Some condiment containers are even shaped like Mickey.

If you want to take some Mickey images home with you, rest assured that you can usually find Hidden Mickeys on items such as souvenir mugs, merchandise bags and boxes, T-shirts, and Christmas tree ornaments sold in the shops. So even when you're far away from the sea, you can continue to enjoy Hidden Mickeys!

Note: There are usually some especially good Hidden Mickeys on the souvenir mugs—tiny and hard to spot. The designs change every couple of years, and every time they come up with a new design, the Hidden Mickeys change.

Notes

CHAPTER 8

My Favorite Hidden Mickeys

•••••••••••••••••••••••••••

In this field guide, I've described more than 300 Hidden Mickeys found on the Disney Cruise Line ships and on Castaway Cay. I enjoy every one of them, but the following are extra special to me. They're special because of their uniqueness, their deep camouflage (which makes them especially hard to find), or the "Eureka!" response they elicit when I spot them—or any combination of the above. Here then are my favorite Hidden Mickeys of the Disney Cruise Line. I apologize to you if your favorite seagoing Hidden Mickey is not (yet) on the list below.

My Top Ten

1. Mickey in the Cadillac Lounge, *Disney Wonder*. On the front wall mural inside the lounge, this tiny classic Mickey in lights is a great example of a Hidden Mickey that's hard to find. (Chap. 5, Clue 40)

2. The full-body rusted-coin Mickey in the Conched Out Bar on Castaway Cay. You have to know where to look to spot this Mickey image. Raise a glass and celebrate when you find him! (Chap. 6, Clue 8)

3. Donald Duck on a pail on the *Disney Magic*. He peers at you from a mural behind the Shore Excursions counter. Cool image of our favorite duck! (Chap. 4, Clue 29)

4. Octopus Mickey in interactive paintings on the *Disney Dream* and *Disney Fantasy*. I saw the image on Deck 10 near the forward elevators. Just stand in front of the painting to activate it and then look for the pink octopus. This is one unique octopus! (Chap. 2, Clue 24 and Chap. 3, Clue 24)

5. Mickeys on wall maps at Guest Services, *Disney Fantasy*. These faint classic Mickeys are among the best map Mickeys you'll ever see. Don't ask for directions! (Chap. 3, Clues 52 and 53)

6. Tiny WaveBands Mickey, *Disney Wonder*. Inside the club, on the floor near the stage, check out this admirable example of a classic Hidden Mickey. Kudos to the artist! (Chap. 5, Clue 39)

7. Peacock-feather classic Mickey, Bon Voyage bar, *Disney Fantasy*. Only one feather on the wall mural behind the bar hides a classic Mickey image. Nice touch! (Chap. 3, Clue 54)

8. Midship Detective Agency Game, *Disney Dream* and *Disney Fantasy*. If you stay alert, you'll spot several Hidden Mickeys during this fun interactive game on ship, among them the tiny, light blue full-body Mickey on the introductory computer screen as you register for the game. Use your game magnifying glass to search for Hidden Images whenever you can! (Chap. 2, Clues 3, 26, and 42 and Chap. 3, Clues 3, 37, and 38)

9. Sorcerer Mickey, Disney's Oceaneer Club, *Disney Magic*. This kid's club on all the Disney ships often has Disney characters outlined in points of light on the ceiling. This one is extra special. It's worth the visit to appreciate the artistry! (Chap. 4, Clue 11)

10. Sunken Mickeys (and Minnie) at Castaway Cay. If you snorkel, explore the snorkeling lagoon to find statues of Mickey and Minnie, as well as classic Mickeys in sunken cement balls. Talk about finding sunken treasure! (Chap. 6, Clues 17 and 18)

Don't Stop Now!

• •

Hidden Mickey mania is contagious. The benign pastime of searching out Hidden Mickeys has escalated into a bona fide vacation mission for many Disney fans. I'm happy to add my name to the list of hunters. Searching for images of the Main Mouse can enhance a solo cruise or a vacation for the entire family. Little ones delight in spotting and greeting Mickey Mouse and other Disney characters on the ships. As children grow, the Hidden Mickey game is a natural evolution of their fondness for the Mouse.

Join the search! With alert eyes and mind, you can spot Hidden Mickey classics as well as new Hidden Mickeys just waiting to be found. Even beginners have happened upon a new, unreported Hidden Mickey or two. As new areas open and older ones get refurbished, new Hidden Mickeys will usually slip in to await discovery.

The Disney entertainment phenomenon is unique in many ways, and Hidden Mickey mania is one manifestation of Disney's universal appeal. Join in the fun! Maybe I'll see you on one of the ships or on Castaway Cay, marveling (like me) at the Hidden Gems. They're waiting patiently for us to discover them.

Notes

Index to Mickey's Hiding Places

For easy look-ups, the Hidden Mickeys in this field guide are indexed by ship and by island. You can search your ship by Deck or by the name of the attraction, restaurant, shop, or other area you're visiting, and you can search Castaway Cay by area or place name. Have a ball!

Note: This Index includes only those places that harbor confirmed Hidden Mickeys. So if the area you're looking for isn't included, Mickey isn't hiding there. Or if he is, I haven't yet spotted him.

Psst! If you leave from Port Canaveral, you can hunt for Hidden Mickeys in the check-in terminal. See page 18 for clues.

– Steve Barrett

Castaway Cay Hiding Places

Castaway Cay (cont'd.)

Disney Dream Hiding Places

By Deck

97

Disney Dream, By Deck (cont'd.)

Disney Dream, By Place

Disney Dream, By Place (cont'd.)

Disney Fantasy Hiding Places

Disney Fantasy, By Deck (cont'd.)

Disney Fantasy, By Place

Disney Fantasy, By Place (cont'd.)

Disney Magic Hiding Places

By Deck

Disney Magic, By Deck (cont'd.)

Disney Magic, By Place

Disney Magic, By Place (cont'd.)

Disney Wonder Hiding Places

By Deck

Disney Wonder, By Deck (cont'd.)

Deck 10, cont'd.

Deck 11

Disney Wonder, By Place

Disney Wonder, by Place (cont'd.)

W